IN THE WORKPLACE

# Health AND Social Care

## GEOFF BARKER

Evans

# Contents

# Working in Health and Social Care

**The healthcare and social work sector concerns the health and wellbeing of people in the community. For many of us, the most familiar aspect of health and social care will be the doctor's surgery, where we go when we feel ill and need treatment. But during the course of our lives, on those occasions when we need help with our physical or our mental health, we may encounter many other people working in this very important area.**

## CARING FOR OTHERS

If you are interested in working in health and social care, there is a huge range of jobs open to you. This book shows a sample of the careers available, from that of doctor, nurse or midwife to children's and young people's services, which concern the welfare and development of younger people on the path to adulthood. For example, education welfare officers offer help to young children and teenagers who are regularly absent from school. They work with the young people to try to get them back into school to continue their education. 'Education' starts at a very early age, however, and the role of nursery school teachers and workers is principally to give children a good start in life and encourage the rounded development of young individuals.

## HEALTHCARE

When patients suffer from illnesses, their condition is often first diagnosed by a doctor. They may then be referred to a health specialist. They will be treated and hopefully will make a quick and full recovery, or they may need some sort of rehabilitation or adjustment to their lifestyle. If the condition is ongoing, they may need to see a number

*A midwife wraps a newborn baby. Midwives play a vitally important role for the family and in the community.*

of health professionals on a regular basis. For example, a diabetic adult may visit a doctor, nurse, optician or optometrist. He or she may even visit a specialist diabetic clinic.

Healthcare workers need to be professional, dedicated, patient and hardworking. They should also have good communication skills and a genuine interest in their patients. Work can be difficult and stressful when patients are weak and vulnerable, and especially when hours are long. However, working in this sector can be extremely rewarding. There are few jobs that deal so closely and intimately with real issues of life, from birth to death – so if you're looking for a career in this field, you need to be mentally tough as well as compassionate. If you think you want to be a nurse, but you're squeamish and faint at the sight of blood, you may need to consider other career options.

### SOCIAL WORK AND SOCIAL CARE

Social work is full of uniquely rewarding jobs. If you feel it may be your role in life to help people encountering a range of mental health issues or physical disabilities, then you should find the right career within social work. This sector requires open-minded individuals who are not quick to judge others but have plenty of patience and good humour. This field also includes social care, where professionals provide specialised personal care by supporting individuals in everyday tasks. Social workers in general must have the ability to get on with and understand other people, but they also need to be able to leave work at the end of the day and not take their professional problems home with them.

**TO WORK IN HEALTH AND SOCIAL CARE, YOU WILL NEED**

●

*'people' skills*

●

*patience*

●

*a tactful and understanding temperament*

●

*strength and resilience*

●

*an open-minded, non-judgemental approach to your work*

*A care worker has a reassuring chat with an older person. Those wishing to work in health and social care should have a genuine interest in people.*

# Working in a Core Healthcare Role

**Healthcare workers are generally concerned with the health and wellbeing of people. There are many familiar core, or key, healthcare roles such as doctor, nurse, surgeon, midwife and paramedic.**

## MEDICAL DOCTORS

Medical doctors gain experience through working in hospitals. Those who stay in hospital medicine go on to specialise in different fields such as accident and emergency (A&E) or anaesthetics. Depending on the medical doctor's special field, the job can vary hugely. General practitioners (or GPs) are family doctors who run a practice or are part of a team of doctors. They perform a vital role in the community – listening to, examining and communicating with patients. They can then diagnose and treat the patient, or refer individuals for specialist treatment.

GPs educate people about healthier lifestyles and help them understand how to prevent and deal with problems. GPs also prescribe medicine to patients. Most doctors use computers every day at work – for storing patient records, looking up test results and keeping up to date with the latest research into medical conditions.

### MAIN TASKS – GENERAL PRACTITIONER
•
*seeing and assessing patients*
•
*arranging suitable tests and interpreting the results*
•
*referring cases for specialist treatment*
•
*reviewing and assessing patients on an ongoing basis*

### TO BECOME A DOCTOR, YOU WILL NEED
•
*a degree in medicine*
•
*good communication skills*
•
*an interest in the wellbeing of patients*
•
*dedication and reliability*
•
*an interest in science and healthcare*

*Many doctors are based in hospitals. Here a doctor assesses a patient's medical condition.*

GPs often have a heavy workload, but need to spend enough time with each patient to make the correct diagnosis.

## Dilip – general practitioner

'I decided to become a doctor when I was about 14. I spent a lot of time with children with disabilities and realised that I was very lucky to be healthy and wanted to help people less fortunate than myself. There are many ways you can help people, but I thought being a doctor was best for me . . . I really enjoyed science and found it fascinating to learn about how the body works.

'I like being able to help when people come in and tell me all the things that are wrong with them. I examine them, arrange tests and put the pieces of the jigsaw together to find out what the problem is, then I'm usually able to help them. I find it very satisfying when I can make people better. Most people come into the surgery with ongoing problems that take time to cure, but sometimes people can be very ill and need to be managed quickly and efficiently. It is important to be prepared for anything when you come into work each day.

'The job can be difficult at times. It can be very hard when you have to tell people bad news, or if they come in very upset about their lives. Sometimes it is difficult to find the right words to say to comfort them. But I find my job very satisfying and interesting . . . I am glad I decided to become a doctor.'

# WORKING AS A NURSE

Nurses (both male and female) care for patients, provide support for patients' families and carers and give advice on health and wellbeing. They need to be excellent communicators as they work so closely with patients, and they form a crucial part of the healthcare team which also includes doctors and physiotherapists. Nursing incorporates a wide range of jobs, but nurses train to specialise within four different areas: adult nursing, children's nursing, mental health nursing or learning disabilities nursing. Nurses either work in hospitals or in the community, where patients can receive nursing care and support from district nurses or health visitors, for example. There are nurses working in schools and occupational health nurses employed in the workplace.

## MAIN TASKS – DISTRICT NURSE

- *visiting patients at their home*
- *assessing and cleaning patients' wounds*
- *providing patient documentation*
- *working with other team members*
- *promoting healthy living and diet*
- *referring patients to other healthcare specialists, if required*

### HANDY HINT

*There are two ways to become a nurse. You can train at a Higher Education Institute (HEI) for three years to obtain a Diploma of Higher Education in Nursing. Alternatively, check out the colleges and universities offering three- or four-year courses for a Bachelor (Hons) degree in Nursing Studies. Both routes involve a split between supervised nursing practice – in a hospital, for example – and theory.*

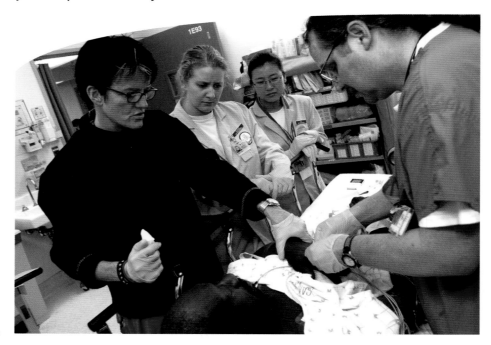

*Nurses carefully assess a man's injuries in the emergency room of a hospital. Student nurses learn quickly by witnessing first-hand real-life cases.*

## Michelle – district nurse (staff community nurse)

'At school I always wanted to be a nurse. My dad was a nurse in the Navy and I used to love listening to all his stories about the job. I wanted to find out more about people – and working with patients seemed such a good way to do it. So after school I did a nursing course for three years. I also worked as a staff nurse in a hospice for a few years. I enjoyed that, but the great thing about doing nursing is that so many options are open to you.

'I definitely made the right decision to change direction slightly and become a district nurse though. I love it. While I was training I had placements in the community with the district nurse team, and it felt like I was learning more with a mentor, on a one-to-one basis. It seemed like such a lovely way to work, thinking on your feet all the time.

'Staff shortages can make the job more difficult, but you still always try to deliver the same level of care to the patients. You have to use communication skills, assessment skills and know how to prioritise. You can knock on someone's door and not quite know what's going to happen next. Also, when you enter someone's house, they're more themselves so that can be more of a challenge sometimes! But I love the patients, even when they're difficult. The patients make the job what it is – this is the only job I want to do.'

*Health visitors spend a large part of their time visiting patients in their home or in residential care homes.*

# WORKING AS A MIDWIFE

Midwives care for mothers and their babies during labour and birth. Most births take place in hospital, although a growing number of mothers give birth at home. Midwives can opt to work alongside hospital or home births. They assist women throughout the birthing process in straightforward cases, only calling a doctor if there are complications. Midwives also help mothers and babies during pregnancy and in the early days of the newborn baby's life.

## HELP IS AT HAND

Midwives hold clinics for expectant mothers and may also run training sessions for pregnant women and their partners. After the birth, a midwife will arrange home visits and is able to offer a range of counselling skills. New mothers may sometimes find breastfeeding difficult, or they may suffer from post-natal depression; some expectant mothers may miscarry. A midwife is there to support women through difficult times.

## MAIN TASKS – MIDWIFE

●

*providing ante-natal clinics*

●

*carrying out post-natal visits*

●

*assisting with births*

●

*helping mothers feel in control*

●

*working with other team members*

●

*providing parenthood classes*

●

*organising aqua-natal classes*

## HANDY HINT

*If you are male and think you would like to become a midwife, you will be in a minority, but it is certainly possible. You will need to be calm and reassuring, and able to empathise, but as long as you have the correct training to look after mother and baby, you can pursue a career in midwifery. You will also need to be sensitive to the fact that some mothers, because of their religion, culture, or simply personal choice, will prefer to have a woman as a midwife.*

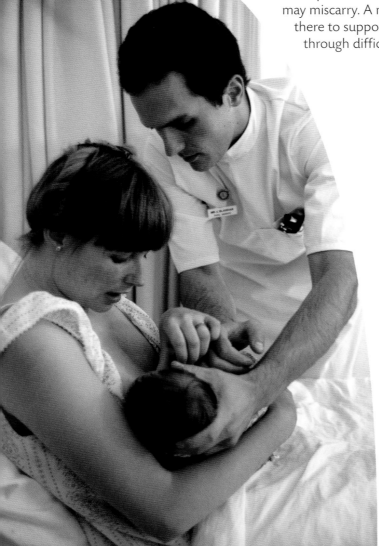

*Most midwives are women, but men can also become midwives. They help teach the skills needed by young mothers to breastfeed, change and bathe their babies.*

*Midwives carry out ante-natal visits, as they check growth at various stages of pregnancy.*

## Anne – community midwife

'My mum was a nurse and I always wanted to be one too . First I did general nursing, which included two months' midwifery. Working with women appealed to me, and initially midwifery was something I thought I'd like to do. Once I'd started the training, I knew it was for me.

'You're in a very privileged position as a midwife. You're invited into people's homes and you get to know the mum-to-be, the family, the children . . . You see them through such a special time – most women only do this once or twice in their lives. I'd probably do the job without pay . . . no, I wouldn't be able to afford to, but that's the way you feel. It's a job you never tire of.

'It can be very upsetting if a pregnant woman loses a baby, but we provide support for mums, so they can talk things through with us. Often you've already built up quite a relationship with them. You need to have a caring nature in this job.

'With home births, you're on call so you must be available to go. When the call comes in, your heart starts going. But when you're at the birth, you have to be calm . . . and you have to be patient. Home births are low risk and things are more relaxed at home.'

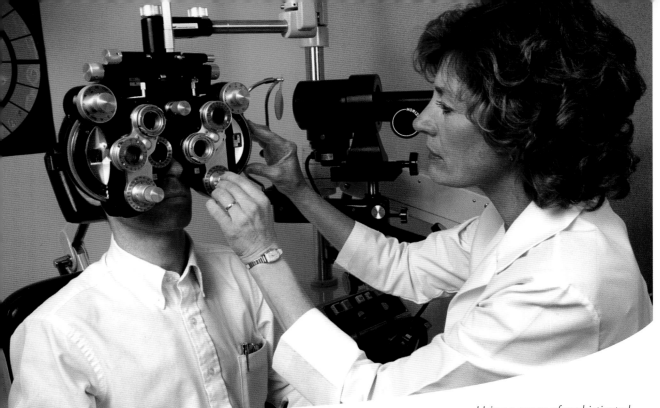

## THE EYES HAVE IT

Another important specialist field in healthcare is concerned with vision, and is known as optometry. There is a range of jobs with quite similar sounding names – optometrist, orthoptist and dispensing optician. Optometrists examine eyes, measuring defective vision and working out a suitable lens prescription; orthoptists diagnose, investigate and treat patients with defective binocular vision, such as a squint; and dispensing opticians do not conduct eye examinations, but interpret eye prescriptions. All professions require good communication skills and a strong interest in science.

## DENTISTRY

Dentistry is an important specialist sector of healthcare concerning not only the teeth, but also the mouth and gums. Dentists diagnose problems of the mouth and aim to prevent tooth decay and gum disease, examining and cleaning patients' teeth and gums, as well as filling, crowning, scaling and extracting teeth where necessary. Teamwork is important as dentists can work closely in the same practice with many other health professionals, such as dental assistants, technicians, nurses, hygienists and therapists.

*Using a range of sophisticated instruments, an optometrist carries out an eye examination. A patient may require glasses to correct an abnormality.*

**HANDY HINT**
*If you want to become a dentist, you will need good science grades at A level and you will need to study hard for five years after that. Find a university with a dental school attached – you will study anatomy, physiology and pathology as well as practical aspects of dentistry. Once you have passed your exams, you will be required to register with the General Dental Council.*

## Jennifer – dental nurse

'I started the job as a dental nurse working just one day a week within a private practice. Then the opportunity came to work at another location, training on the job and going to college. I have just qualified, which is great.

'I like the change of tempo at work. There are times when I'm very busy assisting the dentist with patients, and others when I work alone and get on with jobs to keep the practice up to date. My day is always varied – the unexpected can happen and it is essential to work in a flexible manner. Each day's appointments list is usually pretty full, but there may suddenly be an emergency . . . and you need to book that in as well, so you may be stretched sometimes. The hours can be long and you need good health yourself to function well.

'I work closely with the dentist so it's important to build a good rapport and a way of working that is good for both of you. As a dental nurse, you have to think about the needs of the dentist, the patient, as well as the parent, if the patient is a child.'

*A dental nurse will work closely with the dentist during surgery, making sure that all the instruments are properly sterilised and ready to use.*

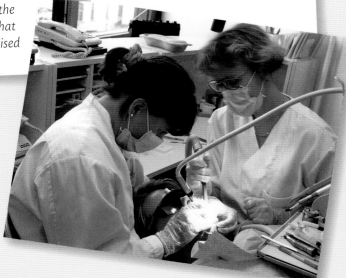

**MAIN TASKS – DENTAL NURSE**
●
*assisting the dentist in the surgery*
●
*making sure the patient is comfortable*
●
*assisting with processing x-ray films*
●
*running the surgery*

## FINDING A JOB – PARAMEDIC

*For this job, you will need to take a short training course to become an ambulance care assistant. After this you will work under supervision for a period of probation and gain experience. Then you will take an intensive training course to qualify as an ambulance technician. You will need to train further to become a paramedic, and you must be at least 21 years of age to do this job.*

*Paramedics respond to medical emergencies and will be present at traffic accidents. They start any necessary treatment.*

# FROM SUPPORT STAFF TO SURGEONS

There are many other vital healthcare professions. Some, such as paramedic and ambulance driver, are very visible roles; others may be more behind the scenes, for example administration worker or healthcare manager. But all healthcare workers play a vital part in the smooth and efficient running of a hospital or health practice. Support workers such as hospital porters move equipment and supplies and ensure that patients are transported to the correct ward. Infections in hospitals are a major threat to patient safety. Sterile services technicians make sure that all hospital instruments, such as needles and scalpels and other equipment, are meticulously clean and safe to use. Specialist surgeons carry out operations on patients with injuries and diseases, or to improve the quality of life for people with conditions that are gradually worsening.

There is a huge range of healthcare roles. If you are a good communicator, work well in a team but have plenty of initiative and are genuinely interested in the welfare of patients, you are likely to find an exciting profession that matches your attributes perfectly.

### EMERGENCY!

Ambulance staff include paramedics, ambulance care assistants and technicians. Drivers can respond fast to an emergency call, arriving at the scene of an accident or at someone's home. Paramedics will examine the patient on site, for example following a road accident,

or after a suspected heart attack. They will then take action, giving the patient immediate, appropriate care or transferring the person to hospital as quickly and as safely as possible. Individuals looking for a career in this field will need to be calm under pressure, able to think on their feet and make the right decisions.

### SMOOTH RUNNING

Receptionists answer telephone calls, make appointments and are there to meet and greet visitors to clinics and hospitals, while health administrators can work within different departments to assist with the running of the offices. Hospitals and other healthcare practices need well maintained health records so that key medical staff can consult files and computer databases and quickly retrieve up-to-date patient information. Health records staff provide this vital service.

Using considerable leadership and communication skills, health service managers are responsible for the smooth running of various health services, ensuring that they are delivered efficiently. Practice managers run GPs' surgeries, financial managers manage budgets and information managers use ICT (information and communication technology) to monitor performance and improve patient care in a hospital, for example. Skilful and experienced managers can become directors and chief executives.

*Mental health service workers assist in administrative duties at a psychiatric centre. They work together in a team.*

### WHERE WILL I BE?
*As a newly qualified doctor, one of the many career paths available might be to become a hospital doctor, or a doctor in a specialist field such as paediatrics. Eventually you might gain a senior role as a consultant.*

# Other Healthcare Jobs

**Alongside the core healthcare professions, there are a lot of other jobs concerned with taking care of people's physical and mental wellbeing. If a doctor thinks a patient needs it, he or she may refer that patient to one of a range of specialists who can help.**

## COUNSELLING

Not all health problems are physical; many are caused by mental health issues. People sometimes need help coping with a difficult short-term problem, such as the loss of a job, or with a longer-term condition, such as depression. Mental health professionals include counsellors, psychotherapists, psychologists and psychiatrists. These terms sometimes cause confusion, as the roles can overlap. Counsellors help people talk about their feelings and behaviour confidentially in a quiet, safe setting. By listening carefully and asking questions, counsellors are able to help people find solutions to their personal problems. In this way, counsellors can help a client handle his or her everyday life better.

### TO BECOME A COUNSELLOR, YOU WILL NEED
●
*listening and observational skills*
●
*patience and sensitivity*
●
*an ability to build trust*

### HANDY HINT
*It is unusual for people to start full-time counselling early in their working lives. Many counselling courses prefer mature students. People who have already worked in nursing, social work or teaching may be well suited to a full-time counselling course because they are likely to have relevant life experience. If you are determined to become a counsellor at an early age, start with a part-time introductory course and contact an official organisation for further advice.*

*People suffering from a particular problem, such as alcoholism or grief after a close relative's death, often find it useful to take part in group therapy.*

A counsellor will encourage a client to talk about her own feelings and listen very carefully.

## Caroline – counsellor

'I was 16 when I left school and I felt lost about what my future would hold. At such a young age, it can be so difficult to know what direction to take. Later, when I was studying for a degree, I met a tutor who inspired me and changed my life. She was trained as a counsellor, and when I was in her class I felt completely connected to what she was teaching. All of a sudden I felt like I understood what I wanted to do with my life. I was still very young to start a counselling course, so I went abroad for two years to gain as much counselling experience as I could. I made a list of my ambitions and set about achieving them. I was accepted on to one of the best counselling courses in the country and continued my journey to becoming a counsellor.

'As a counsellor, you create an honest and respectful relationship with your client. It is a privilege for someone to share his or her deepest feelings with you. Counselling is a difficult job because you have to work at the client's pace and not to hold judgement about what you hear. Sometimes a client shares something that reminds you of a personal issue you have not resolved yourself – and that is when you need to look at your personal response within your own counselling.'

*Music therapists can work in a variety of settings, including hospices for the terminally ill. Therapists help families by making the end of patients' lives more enjoyable.*

# ALL SORTS OF THERAPY

There is a wide variety of therapists within the healthcare sector. An art therapist can help someone with learning difficulties express his or her feelings through art. A speech and language therapist can help patients with communication problems and eating, drinking and swallowing disorders. A music therapist can use music and sound to help someone with mental health problems or behavioural difficulties. These therapists work very closely with other professionals, including nurses, physiotherapists, psychologists, social workers and teachers, as well as occupational therapists.

### GAINING CONFIDENCE

An occupational therapist's job involves the kinds of things that 'occupy' people every day (including looking after themselves, working and relaxing). Occupational therapists help people with physical, mental or social problems to gain more control and confidence. Along with other members of the health and social care team, occupational therapists enable their clients to make the most of their abilities so that they live as complete a life as possible.

### FINDING SMART SOLUTIONS

If, for example, an older woman with arthritis is struggling to fill a kettle for a cup of tea, an occupational therapist can work out a solution. This might involve installing special equipment in the woman's home or adapting the client's kitchen to suit her needs. The therapist would devise a different plan of action for different situations, for example, if a person is suffering from Alzheimer's disease. Occupational therapists can work in hospitals, hospices, residential homes, GP practices, schools, colleges or prisons to look after the needs of a wide range of clients. Part-time and flexible work, as well as private practice, is also possible.

**TO BECOME AN OCCUPATIONAL THERAPIST, YOU WILL NEED**

●

*a genuine interest in people*

●

*a caring nature*

●

*adaptability and resourcefulness*

## Alice – occupational therapist

'What I enjoy about being an occupational therapist is also what can often make my job a difficult and demanding one, but it is never boring or repetitive! Every person I work with has his or her own difficulties – from the young child who has a clumsy gait (walking pattern) and finds school life difficult to the elderly adult who relies on a wheelchair to get around and needs advice to redesign her kitchen. My job is to assist and enable individuals to achieve their maximum level of independence and functioning. This is challenging as every one of us has different ideas, goals, family support, and living environments that affect what we want to achieve in life. For a person with a disability, what we would consider minor actions, such as putting on socks and shoes, can be a major achievement.

'One of the attractions of the job is the different individuals we work with, plus the variety of working environments such as hospitals, schools, people's own homes and work situations. When people disregard your advice or have no desire to achieve agreed goals, the job can be frustrating. But what's great about it is that there is huge scope for "job satisfaction".'

An occupational therapist can assess a patient's movement skills using a peg board.

21

## PHARMACISTS

Pharmacists are experts on the use of medicine. Hospital pharmacists' work includes dispensing medicine to patients and managing the hospital's pharmacy services. Many pharmacists work in community pharmacies (from healthcare centres to high-street chemists and large supermarkets); they prepare certain medicines and dispense drugs to members of the public. Other pharmacists work for private companies in the pharmaceutical industry. All pharmacists need to be good at science, accurate, methodical and responsible.

## FINDING A JOB – PHARMACIST

*If you are interested in becoming a pharmacist, you need to obtain good A level grades in English, maths and science (with chemistry and biology as the preferred options). You then need to obtain a degree in pharmacy. Decide whether you want to work in a hospital, laboratory or in the community (retail or healthcare). Carry out research into jobs by looking in medical publications, on the internet, or in local newspapers. Ask health professionals and your local pharmacists about work in your area.*

## RADIOGRAPHERS

Radiographers work mainly in hospital imaging departments, accident and emergency departments and operating theatres, using x-rays, ultrasound and other sophisticated equipment to produce images of human organs and limbs. A patient visiting the A&E department in a hospital with a suspected fractured wrist would be seen by a radiographer, who would take an x-ray to aid diagnosis and treatment.

## PHYSIOTHERAPISTS

Physiotherapists treat patients suffering from a wide range of injuries, illnesses and conditions. They massage and manipulate soft tissue, and recommend exercises to improve a patient's mobility. Many physiotherapists receive referrals from other healthcare professionals or are recommended by a satisfied customer.

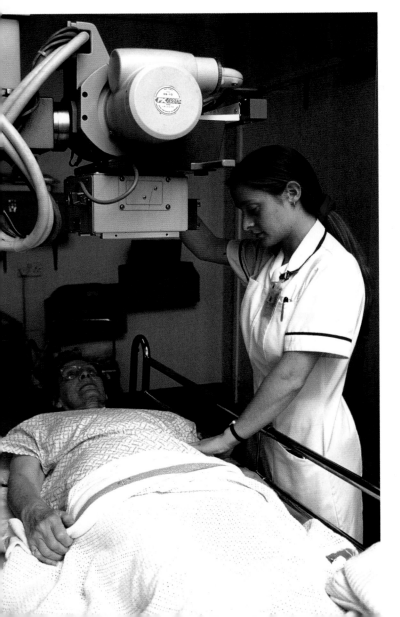

*A radiographer will assess a patient's needs before using imaging equipment. An x-ray will help diagnose the problem.*

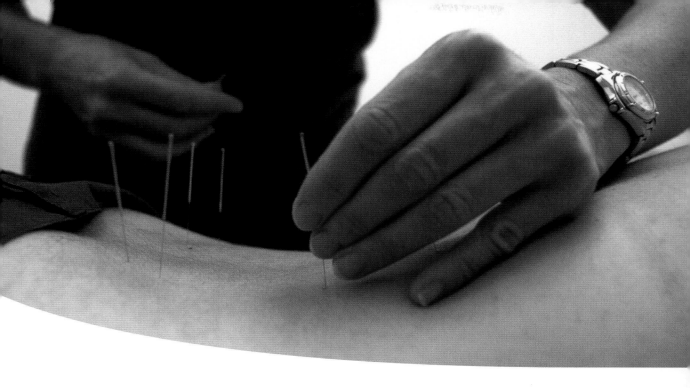

## COMPLEMENTARY THERAPY

There are careers within healthcare that do not fit neatly into the traditional framework of medicine as we know it. These are often referred to as 'complementary therapies'. Many patients find complementary therapies a useful alternative and some of them are now used alongside more traditional methods. Complementary therapists include osteopaths, chiropractors, acupuncturists, massage practitioners, reflexologists and homeopaths.

An osteopath uses a holistic approach to the human body and tries to relieve pain and correct abnormalities using manipulation. Patients may be referred to osteopaths by GPs, but usually they visit an osteopath as the result of personal recommendation. Chiropractors treat problems with joints, bones and muscles and use their hands on the body's joints – in particular the spine – to make focused adjustments to improve function. Acupuncturists use an ancient form of Chinese medicine to heal. They examine patients carefully and find out their medical history before inserting needles into the skin to stimulate key points and regulate the entire body.

Like traditional health workers, complementary therapists need to have good communication skills and should inspire trust in their patients and other healthcare professionals. They also need manual dexterity. For certain disciplines, such as osteopathy, training can take as long as five years. Once qualified, most complementary therapists become self-employed.

*An acupuncturist inserts fine needles into a patient's skin. Acupuncturists use a holistic approach to healing, and treat imbalances in the body.*

**WHERE WILL I BE?**
*As an occupational therapist, one possible career path could begin with a job as a support worker, where you would qualify by receiving in-service training. Alternatively you could study part- or full-time to degree level. For qualified occupational therapists, there are many opportunities to progress to research, teaching or management positions.*

# Social Work

**Social workers support vulnerable groups in society, such as children and families, people with physical disabilities and those with mental health problems. They assess people's needs and try to find lasting solutions to problems they may have.**

## WORK INVOLVING CHILDREN

Social workers tend to specialise within a particular field, for example, in the care and protection of children. Work of this type can be stressful, as children may have been abused by their parents or carers, physically, emotionally or sexually. Social workers visit children and their families in the home, or may escort children on visits to their parents or family if they are being looked after elsewhere. A social worker may have to make the decision that an abused child should be removed from his or her parents. In this case, the social worker then has to help find a new home for the child.

### MAIN TASKS – SOCIAL WORKER

- *assessing situations and individuals' needs*
- *organising support*
- *developing relationships with individuals and family*
- *working with other professionals*
- *writing reports, records and letters*
- *attending court hearings*

### HANDY HINT
*It's important to be able to empathise with the problems of children and families. As social work can be very stressful, one of the most important qualities in a social worker is the ability to leave the job behind and 'switch off' at the end of the day.*

*A social worker has to develop trust quickly with people. Workers may use props like dolls to try to work out if a child has suffered abuse.*

A social worker interviews a father and his children at home. Social workers must handle pressure, as they will have difficult situations to face.

## Scott – social worker (child protection)

'The thing I enjoy most about my job is the sheer variety. You never know what challenges you will have to deal with when you first arrive at the office. They could range from carrying out a joint interview with the police, doing an assessment for a child with disabilities or supervising contact with a parent and her or his children. As a "duty" social worker, a significant amount of my job is child protection. I spend two to three days a week on duty, and this involves taking calls from both the public and professionals. This can be daunting sometimes, as often we have little information on families and our assessments need to be as thorough as possible to ensure the best outcome for the child. Working together with police, health and education colleagues is another key element of social work. You definitely need to have good listening skills and the ability to stick with people when the going gets tough.

'If we don't have enough resources we can't always provide a proper service for clients. This can obviously be frustrating for both worker and service user. Doing all the paperwork is time consuming, but it's important to keep up-to-date records. When the job gets really difficult, I find a good sense of humour helps.'

### FOSTERING AND ADOPTION

Social workers in the fostering and adoption sector assess whether couples or families are going to make suitable carers for children who have lost their parents or been removed from their care. Social workers can help find a short- or long-term solution for children with a foster family, or in a permanent home with people who are willing to adopt. Social workers can also provide support for families who agree to foster or adopt a child.

# MENTAL HEALTH WORKERS

Social workers who specialise in the mental health sector work with people with a range of mental health needs. For example, a social worker may be assigned to an older person with memory problems following the onset of Alzheimer's disease or a young adult suffering from depression or schizophrenia. Mental health workers assess their clients' different needs and try to help them adapt and cope with everyday life. They may visit clients every day to help make meals and check medication. Social workers have the power to remove people from their homes if they are likely to be a danger to themselves or others in their family or the community.

*Mental health workers work as a team to look after a man in a nursing home. Workers need to have a compassionate nature to help people.*

### TO BECOME A MENTAL HEALTH WORKER, YOU WILL NEED

●

*a real interest in people's welfare*

●

*excellent communication skills*

●

*the ability to handle pressure*

### HANDY HINT

*If you are interested in working in the mental health sector, study subjects such as health and social care, psychology, sociology and ICT at school.*

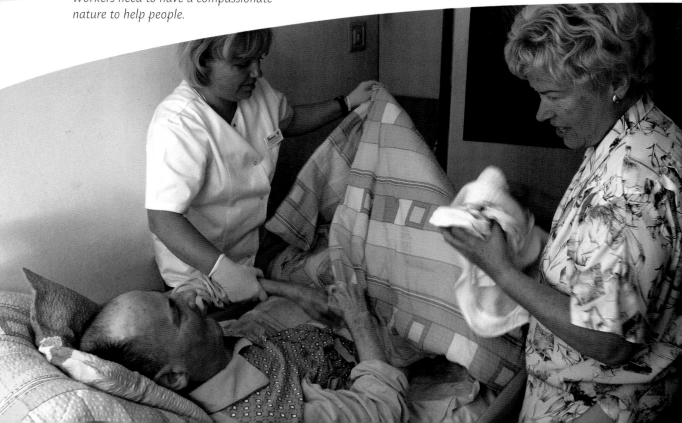

A mental health worker can help a client learn new skills, such as how to use a computer.

## Tyler – mental health worker

'I work with people who have all sorts of different mental health needs. When I go into someone's home, I assess what type of help they need. We then try to support them and give them a chance to live independently in their own homes.

'I studied to become a social worker and quickly realised that I wanted to specialise in mental health care. My grandfather had Alzheimer's for many years and I think that experience made me want to help other people cope with mental health disorders. I'm outgoing and enjoy working with different people. As well as clients, I also work with psychiatric nurses and psychiatrists, monitoring and reviewing people with mental health problems. Friends have told me I'm good at problem-solving . . . I think this helps in the job too. It's important not to judge people as well.

'There can be plenty of paperwork and updating of records on the computer. I much prefer the hands-on time I have working with clients, but I have to balance this with time in the office. You also have to keep up to speed with any developments in mental health – the government might introduce a new policy or way of working. Social work is hard but I find it rewarding, as you can make a difference to someone's life.'

*Probation officers need to be able to present information. A probation officer gives a lecture on the dangers of reckless driving to young offenders.*

# YOUTH AND COMMUNITY WORKERS

Youth and community workers help young people to grow, learn and develop as individuals, and encourage them to play a positive role in their community. They might work in a school, youth club, community centre, church or mosque. Here they help young people organise projects or activities, such as a trip to an outward bound centre.

## CRIMINAL JUSTICE SERVICES

Other community workers are employed within the criminal justice services sector. Social workers in this field include probation officers and probation service officers. Although their roles are different, both work to protect the public and promote community safety.

Probation officers' work of crime prevention and promotion of safety within the community involves working with offenders and prisoners during and after their sentences. The probation officer will draw up a report when an offender attends court, looking at family and education. The officer meets the offender and his or her family and identifies the individual's needs and the risks. The probation officer works out a plan to help prevent the person re-offending and continues to assess the offender and his or her potential risk to the public.

## FINDING A JOB
*If you'd like to become a social worker, a good way to gain vital experience is to do voluntary work in a social care or community setting. If you like the work, you can then train to be a social worker. A three-year degree in social work will combine study with plenty of practical experience. Decide which sector of social work you are most likely to enjoy. Are you more suited to working with children and families, the elderly, people with mental health problems or those with physical disabilities? Or maybe you prefer to work with offenders? Once you have completed your training in social work, there should be plenty of job opportunities.*

## TO BECOME A PROBATION OFFICER, YOU WILL NEED

●

*the ability to work in a team*

●

*patience and firmness*

●

*a genuine interest in helping people*

●

*an understanding of criminal law*

### ONE-TO-ONE

Probation officers supervise offenders if there is a custodial sentence. They also manage offenders sentenced with a community or court order, making sure that offenders follow orders of the court, such as unpaid work for the community. It can be a difficult job building a one-to-one relationship with an offender, as the probation officer will need to try to strike a balance between firmness and helping the offender to develop self-respect.

Probation service officers tend to supervise low-risk offenders. Their job is to support offenders serving community and custodial sentences. To help change offenders' behaviour, they will oversee rehabilitation programmes for people in custody and after release. They may also provide a supporting role to victims of crime and their families.

*Probation officers may decide to recommend a team-building course as part of a rehabilitation programme for young offenders.*

## MAIN TASKS – SUBSTANCE MISUSE WORKER

- *assessing new referrals*
- *developing and implementing care plans with clients*
- *developing trust with clients*
- *providing ongoing evaluation of clients' needs*
- *working with other agencies*
- *maintaining accurate records*

*Substance misuse workers can provide education and one-to-one advice to young people who have become dependent on alcohol.*

### REHABILITATION

Social workers in rehabilitation try to help restore a person's skills and make the most of their abilities. Rehabilitation programmes exist to help a variety of people. Criminal offenders may need rehabilitation to assist their return into the community, while people with hearing impairment or partial sight may need help developing their abilities to cope with everyday life.

### DRUG AND ALCOHOL PROBLEMS

Social workers may specialise in rehabilitation for individuals with substance misuse problems, or addiction to drugs or alcohol. For example, substance misuse workers can help clients who have recently been 'detoxed' from drugs or alcohol, or who are on a detox programme. Workers will help draw up a care plan for people who are in the process of trying to address their problem, and will help to provide one-to-one, group and volunteer support. They often work together with other professionals in healthcare, social care and criminal justice teams. They have to work hard to win substance misusers' trust and they give constructive support, education and guidance.

### WHERE WILL I BE?
*From social worker, you can progress to become a senior social worker or a team manager. Alternatively, you might decide to opt for self-employment as a counsellor or therapist.*

*Vinnie Marino, a former drug addict, teaches a yoga class. Channelling energy in a creative way can help addicts to recover.*

## Caroline – substance misuse worker

'I just love the diversity of the job – no two days are the same. I find working with people a challenge and enjoy helping them to learn more about themselves and how they can affect change in their lives by looking at the choices they make. You need to be able to listen, but sometimes it's also important in this job to challenge their views respectfully. Sometimes the level of non-attendance of the client group we work with is frustrating, even though I am aware that this seems to come with the job. You do need to have patience.

'By far the most challenging aspect of the job is ensuring that goals set for the client are his or her own goals, and not influenced by workers' own values or beliefs.

'My previous jobs have been as a psychiatric nurse. I have always been intrigued by how people behave and interact. I became interested in the field of addiction while working in the psychiatric wards. I like the idea that everyone has the ability to change for the better with the right support. I don't hold the view that being addicted to a substance means an individual has failed. It only means they've made the wrong choices . . . and those choices can be reversed.'

# Social Care

**Workers in social care provide quality personal care and support for people with various practical, social and emotional needs. They work in many different settings, including nursing homes and children's residential units. They also work in people's own homes to help them maintain their independence.**

## RESIDENTIAL CARE

Residential care workers provide vital hands-on care in residential homes or secure institutions for people in need of 24-hour care (on a long-term or temporary basis). They may help children or young adults with physical disabilities or mental health problems, or provide assistance to older people unable to continue living in their own home. Work varies hugely depending on the setting and the people cared for. Sometimes residential care workers will help people carry out practical, day-to-day tasks such as getting dressed. At other times they may give encouragement and support, or sit and listen carefully to a person's problems. Residential care workers do not necessarily need to live in the home themselves; some go there to work, and leave at the end of the working day. Residential care workers include resource workers and care assistants.

**TO BE A RESIDENTIAL CARE MANAGER, YOU WILL NEED**

•

*good communication skills*

•

*a positive outlook*

•

*patience and empathy*

•

*a genuine desire to provide care*

*A residential care manager tries to make sure that each resident is as comfortable and happy as possible.*

**MAIN TASKS – RESIDENTIAL CARE MANAGER**

•

*selecting and training staff*

•

*recording and reviewing patient notes*

•

*supervising medication*

•

*supporting and involving families*

•

*communicating with outside agencies*

•

*keeping up-to-date records on computer*

•

*working out and maintaining rotas on computer*

*A member of staff in a care home reads with a resident who suffers from dementia.*

## David – residential care manager

'Having had plenty of nursing and care experience with older people, I now hold a position of great responsibility as a residential care manager, maintaining the standards of care for 35 residents and the welfare of very hard-working care staff.

'A difficult part of my job involves dealing with the deaths that occur. We get to know the people in our care and become close to them and their families. We are very much like one large family living in a large house, so usually everyone is affected when someone dies. I look after the families (and staff who may not have experienced death) because they may need lots of support. It may be a very sad time but it is also a time when we work very closely together to support and care for one another as a team. I try to use it as a learning experience so that we can improve the care for the next person we support.

'Although I work about 60 hours each week, I enjoy every moment, whether I am providing medication, dealing with wounds, carrying out reviews in hospital or listening to our residents telling me about their life. It is the challenge of ensuring that those who have chosen to spend their remaining years at the nursing home receive the best treatment possible that makes my job worthwhile.'

## CARE AT HOME

Home carers and home care assistants provide special assistance to older clients or people with physical disabilities in their own homes. Depending on the clients' needs, home carers visit their homes up to three or four times a day, making sure that they feed themselves properly and helping with other tasks around the home. The work is likely to involve household chores, such as washing up, emptying bins and making beds. Home carers may also help clients have a bath or they may supervise their medication. The carer's role is to try to ensure that people can live as independently as possible in their own home.

## ORGANISING HOME CARE

Home care organisers assess an individual's needs as well as his or her financial circumstances. They assess whether someone is eligible for support or not, then help to arrange home care to cover specific needs. Home care organisers provide training and give support to carers. Most people working in the field of home care are employed by local authorities or by private care agencies.

### MAIN TASKS – HOME CARER

●

*providing assistance and care for clients*

●

*helping with bathing or showering*

●

*making meals or preparing food*

●

*carrying out other household tasks*

●

*listening to clients*

●

*carrying out first aid, if necessary*

### TO BE A HOME CARER, YOU WILL NEED

●

*patience and a calm approach*

●

*generosity of spirit*

●

*sensitivity*

*A home carer will need to be able to empathise with people who may become upset or frustrated. She will also help with day-to-day practicalities.*

Home carers provide a great service for many older people. Their support helps those who like their independence.

### Berenice – home carer

'I love that I can make just a little difference to people's lives. You don't need to have worked in care before but I think you must have a heart. Sometimes laughter is what people want to hear – it's no use going in all glum as this will only depress people . . . and that's not what this job is about.

'With caring you do become attached to people, especially when you work with them two or three times a day. It can be a bit of a rollercoaster at times especially with clients with mental issues, as they have their good and bad days. You have to look at the person, not their disability. When your clients get ill or pass away it can be very emotional as you do bond with them, and unless you are totally heartless, you grieve.

'It's great to encourage clients to do things about the house, like making a cup of tea, baking a cake or planting some bulbs in the garden. All these things keep them physically active . . . and it helps to keep their mind active too. I go shopping with some, which gives them a great boost, as they don't have to rely on their families for help. We give so little but get so much back. It's a very rewarding job.'

*Day-care officers help with duties such as serving tea to older people at a drop-in centre. Officers look after the welfare of the people and are always there for a chat.*

## DAY-CARE CENTRES

Social care jobs also involve looking after older people at day-care centres. People tend to arrive at the centres during the morning, then they have lunch and leave during the afternoon. Day-care officers help people with practical daily activities, such as taking a bath or going to the toilet. They also organise social activities such as games and trips out.

Day-care officers need to be able to get on well with people from many different backgrounds. They also need a flexible approach to their work, so that they can cope when sudden changes are necessary or if there's an emergency. A trip out from the centre can be fun for members but needs to be very well organised, with the right amount of staff and alternative plans in case things do not run as smoothly as expected.

## FINDING A JOB

*If you are interested in becoming a care assistant, start by contacting a local day-care centre or care agency. Volunteer to help as an unpaid worker and be willing to assist in any capacity – for example, by helping to organise a trip out. Once you have some experience, you will know better if this work suits you. Enquire if there are any opportunities for work as a paid care assistant.*

## HANDY HINT

*If you think you have the right personal qualities to be a carer, see if you can shadow one in their job. This well help you get a measure of the type of work involved. The work may be more physically demanding than you realise, and a single carer may need help with a person who is fairly immobile. In such cases, carers work in pairs and use special equipment such as hoists and curved 'banana boards' to transfer people from one place to another.*

*Sheltered accommodation is a good option for some older people. Residential wardens help the residents.*

## RAISING THE ALARM

There are social care workers, known as residential wardens or by other job titles such as scheme managers, who work in a range of accommodation. Often employed by local authorities, charities and housing associations, they look after fairly independent people living in sheltered accommodation who need a little extra help or support. They may be there to keep an eye on elderly people or disabled individuals, and are typically on hand at the end of an alarm. Some wardens and scheme managers have responsibility for a group of warden-controlled buildings. Other wardens work for universities and colleges and are there to provide practical help or emotional support for young students living away from home.

## WHERE WILL I BE?

*If you are interested in a career in home care, one of the routes you might follow is first to become a home care assistant and then a home carer. From here you could progress to become a senior home carer or home care manager. You could even take the plunge and set up your own care agency.*

# Children's and Young People's Services

**Childcare is an increasingly important service as more and more parents go out to work. Childcare provision includes professionals in playworking, education welfare and early years' education settings, such as nurseries.**

## NURSERY WORKERS

Nursery workers are involved in early years' education. Their jobs vary according to their setting and responsibilities. For example, a nursery school teacher might work in nursery classes and pre-schools, teaching children between the ages of three and five. Nursery workers generally look after children from birth to about seven years of age. They plan and organise a wide variety of early learning activities to develop children's social, emotional, physical and creative abilities. By involving children as individuals and in groups, nursery workers encourage learning through play, practical skills and reading. They also promote good behaviour and make sure children are safe in their nurseries, pre-schools and infant classes. Nursery workers are also employed in hospitals, workplace nurseries and crèches, and work in private family homes and hotels as 'nannies'.

### TO BECOME A NURSERY SCHOOL TEACHER, YOU WILL NEED

- *a love of children*
- *creativity and imagination*
- *excellent communication and listening skills*
- *the ability to work as part of a team*

### MAIN TASKS – NURSERY WORKER

- *planning individual and group activities*
- *supporting young children in their learning through play and activities*
- *creating opportunities for role play, games, singing etc.*
- *encouraging confidence and independence of children*
- *ensuring children's safety*
- *promoting positive behaviour*

*Nursery workers can help young children to develop and learn in a happy and safe environment.*

Nursery school teachers also work with smaller numbers of children whenever possible to establish closer bonds.

## May – nursery school teacher

'I love the variety and flexibility of the job, combining child-centred and adult-planned activities and supporting a child's learning through play. I have different groups in the morning and the afternoon, with girls and boys of three to five, at all stages of development. Each group has up to ten children and each child is assigned a key worker. This enables the worker to get to know the child individually and build a relationship with the child and his or her parents.

'The job is physically and mentally demanding and involves daily planning, keeping written records of observations and photos for each child, and always ensuring that the child has resources to extend and challenge his or her learning through play. I love to see the children develop. They start nursery life as little extensions of their mums and dads, and by the time they leave to go to primary school, they're more confident and independent individuals. It's fascinating to watch a child's development. They learn the most in their first five years. Our activities at nursery are challenging – it's like planting a seed and watching it develop. I have a real pride in the children and I try to treat them as I would my own. I find the job very rewarding and satisfying.'

## PLAYWORKERS

A playworker's job involves planning and supervising play opportunities for children and young people in their leisure time. Playworkers usually work before or after school, at weekends and during school holidays, so most of the jobs tend to be part-time or seasonal. Playworkers give children the chance to experiment through play, either in or out of the usual school setting. Other locations for playwork might be youth clubs, leisure or community centres, church halls, adventure playgrounds or play buses.

The demand for playworkers is likely to continue in the future, as an increasing number of parents look for flexible childcare options while they work. Employers include local authorities, voluntary and charitable organisations, children's party companies and holiday play schemes.

## FINDING A JOB

*If you are interested in becoming a playworker, try to gain some experience of working with children, especially in larger groups. Offer 'babysitting' services to friends and family and contact voluntary and charitable organisations, play providers and children's party companies for possible openings. Research jobs through local and national papers, and the internet and look on council websites for advertisements for playworker jobs.*

*Playworkers try to encourage children to take risks in a safe environment such as an adventure playground.*

## MAIN TASKS – PLAYWORKER

●

*organising groups of children for games*

●

*preparing craft activities*

●

*supervising children at all times*

●

*providing children with a safe environment*

●

*monitoring and evaluating play sessions and events*

●

*encouraging children to experiment through play*

●

*promoting good behaviour in children*

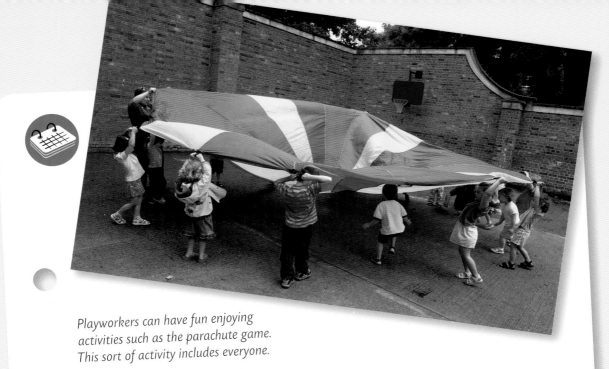

Playworkers can have fun enjoying
activities such as the parachute game.
This sort of activity includes everyone.

### Katrina – playworker

'After leaving school I did four years of fairly meaningless jobs, then I
volunteered as a mothers' help which made me realise I wanted to work
with children. I started to look for a job with children locally. I found a
job working in a children's nursery and started my childcare training. I'd
been working in this sort of environment for about two years, but I
began to find it a bit restrictive and longed for something different.
Around the same time an opportunity became available to volunteer as
a playworker for a local charity. I enjoyed it so much that when a paid
position came up, I applied straight away. I got the job, and have been
working as a playworker ever since.

'As I run open access play sessions I never know how well attended
they will be, which makes it hard to prepare for, but this adds to the
variety of the job. It's harder when young people show challenging
behaviour as this can spoil other children's enjoyment. But I really like
working with a wide range of age groups in my job, outdoors and in all
sorts of locations. I also enjoy playing and being creative with the
children I work with.'

## EDUCATION WELFARE OFFICERS

Many children and young people have serious problems at home, which can affect their lives and the lives of other students and teachers at school. Some children get bullied within the school itself. Education welfare officers and educational psychologists have important roles, within a varied team of professionals, to focus on the happiness and wellbeing of pupils.

Education welfare officers work with schools to help resolve problems of attendance in pupils. If a child or young person is not attending school regularly, an education welfare officer can act as a link to discuss concerns between the school, the pupil and the parents or carers. Education welfare officers also work closely with health advisers, educational psychologists, teachers and police officers. They address issues that arise, for example when children and young people are frequently absent or at risk of exclusion from school. They try to get to the bottom of the problem and help the pupil return to school.

### MAIN TASKS – EDUCATION WELFARE OFFICER

●

*assessing problems and working on solutions*

●

*sharing information with fellow professionals*

●

*trying to improve links between school and home*

●

*supporting excluded pupils on return to school*

●

*writing reports on cases*

●

*giving evidence in court*

*Education welfare officers can assess any problems in the home.*

### WHERE WILL I BE?

*If you are interested in a career working with young children, think about training to become a nursery school teacher. With experience, you could then rise to the position of senior nursery school teacher or head of department and eventually head of a nursery school. Alternatively, you could look into running your own private nursery or playgroup.*

*An education welfare officer keeps an open mind as he tries to establish trust with a young person.*

## Pete – education welfare officer

'I like the challenge of making and maintaining relationships with young people to try to support them in resolving their difficulties. We offer lots of advice and support to parents and carers on managing young people's behaviour and in communicating with them. Many of the parents to whom we offer support lack the experience and quite often the will to bring up their children in appropriate ways. I particularly enjoy the challenge of relating to adolescents, who I feel are the most misunderstood group in society. You have to have a positive regard for others and be able to separate out people from their behaviour, because these two things can be completely different.

'In any work like this you have to accept that there are some things you can do very little about. That's hard sometimes and you tend to carry those issues around with you. Some young people's difficulties are due to poor role modelling by adults, at home as well as in school, and adolescents are often the "victims" of people judging them. I think we need to build trust and develop our understanding of people with difficulties . . . only then can we provide proper support to try to resolve difficulties in a real and lasting way. I believe this type of work is more of a vocation than a job – I really couldn't see myself doing anything else.'

# Further Information

## BOOKS

Blundell, Adrian, Richard Harrison and Benjamin Turney **The Essential Guide to Becoming a Doctor**, Blackwell Publishing, 2007

Gray, Philip **The Penguin Careers Guide**, Penguin, 2008

Hodgson, Susan (ed.) **A-Z of Careers and Jobs**, Kogan Page, 2008

Horner, Nigel **What is Social Work?: Context and Perspectives (Transforming Social Work Practice)**, Learning Matters Ltd, 2006

Lee, George and Olivier Picard **Medical School Interviews: A Practical Guide to Help You Get That Place at Medical School – Over 150 Questions Analysed**, ISC Medical, 2006

Lore, Nicholas and Anthony Spadafore **Now What? The Young Person's Guide to Choosing the Perfect Career**, Fireside Books, 2008

Miller, Lisa **Counselling Skills for Social Work**, Sage Publications Ltd, 2005

## WEBSITES

**http://careersadvice.direct.gov.uk/ helpwithyourcareer/jobprofiles**
A site with a section about the range of professions within Social Services and Medicine and Nursing directories.

**www.alec.co.uk**
A website with general advice and information on careers. Includes tips on writing a CV, finding a job, handling an interview, as well as plenty of careers advice.

**www.careers-guide.com/industry-choices/ medicine-nursing.htm**
General information including careers advice on medicine and nursing.

**www.connexions-direct.com**
A website with invaluable information and advice for young people, including useful database of professions (jobs4u) within 'job families'.

**www.socialcarecareers.co.uk**
Department of Health website with social care and social work careers information.

# Glossary

**adoption**  a legal undertaking to create a parent-child relationship between people not related by blood

**Alzheimer's disease**  a disease of the brain, where the memory and judgement gets worse, leading to dementia

**anaesthetics**  a branch of medicine using drugs to produce the temporary loss of feeling or sensation

**ante-natal**  happening before birth

**aqua-natal**  a safe and gentle exercise class in a swimming pool for women during and after pregnancy

**banana board**  the name for special equipment used to make it easier to lift patients from bed to bed

**binocular vision**  the ability to focus on an object with both eyes to create a single image

**complementary therapy** a type of healing practised by therapists who treat the person as a whole and try to restore the body's natural balance. Therapies include osteopathy, massage and reflexology

**counselling**  listening to people's problems and helping them to resolve them in a structured way

**court order**  a special ruling by a judge

**crèche**  a day nursery for very young children

**custodial sentence**  being sentenced to prison or a period of rehabilitation

**database**  a collection of information, especially computer records

**degenerate**  to get worse

**detox**  short for detoxification, the process of removing toxins or poisons from the body

**dexterity**  physical skill, especially of the hands

**diagnose**  to identify a disease or condition by examining the symptoms

**documentation**  paperwork or documents

**empathise**  the ability to understand and engage with others' feelings

**exclusion**  being refused access

**foster parents**  people who care for children and young people who have been removed from their biological parents

**holistic**  treating as a whole

**homeopath**  a therapist who uses homeopathy (the method of treating illness using a tiny amount of a drug that would normally produce symptoms similar to the effects of the illness)

**hospice**  a home for people in care, especially terminally ill patients

**labour**  the process of giving birth

**manipulation**  treating manually

**paediatrics**  the branch of medicine dealing with the care of infants and children

**pharmaceutical industry** the drug industry, or manufacture of medicines

**post-natal depression** feelings of extreme gloom following childbirth

**prescription**  a document written by a healthcare professional such as a doctor or optometrist

**probation**  a trial period; a court system that deals with offenders by placing them under the supervision of a probation officer

**psychiatrist**  a doctor trained in treating various mental disorders

**psychology**  the scientific study of all forms of human behaviour

**psychotherapist** someone trained to help others in the problems of living by treating their mental well-being

**referral**  someone transferred from the care of one health professional to another

**reflexologist**  a therapist who uses reflexology (squeezing parts of the feet or hands for benefits elsewhere in the body)

**rehabilitation**  helping a patient re-adapt to society

**role play**  acting a role, as part of a process of helping people recover from trauma or difficulties

**schizophrenia**  mental illness characterised by deteriorating personality

**sheltered accommodation**  housing for older, disabled or vulnerable people

**sociology**  the study of human social behaviour

**surgeon**  a doctor who specialises in surgery

**surgery**  a doctor's or dentist's office; or a period during which a doctor or dentist treats patients

**therapist**  someone who treats disorders or disease

**truancy**  being absent from school without permission

**ultrasound**  using ultrasonic waves in medical diagnosis and therapy

**voluntary**  performed willingly, without being paid

**welfare**  well-being; health and happiness

# Index